ABC See, Hear, Do
WRITING PRACTICE

UPPERCASE LETTERS

by Stefanie Hohl

Playful Learning Press

www.abcseeheardo.com

ABC See, Hear, Do Level 1: Writing Practice, Uppercase Letters

Copyright © 2021 by Stefanie Hohl

Summary: A writing workbook to practice writing the uppercase letters of the alphabet. Includes characters from *ABC See, Hear, Do Level 1: Learn to Read Uppercase Letters*.

ISBN 978-1-63824-010-5

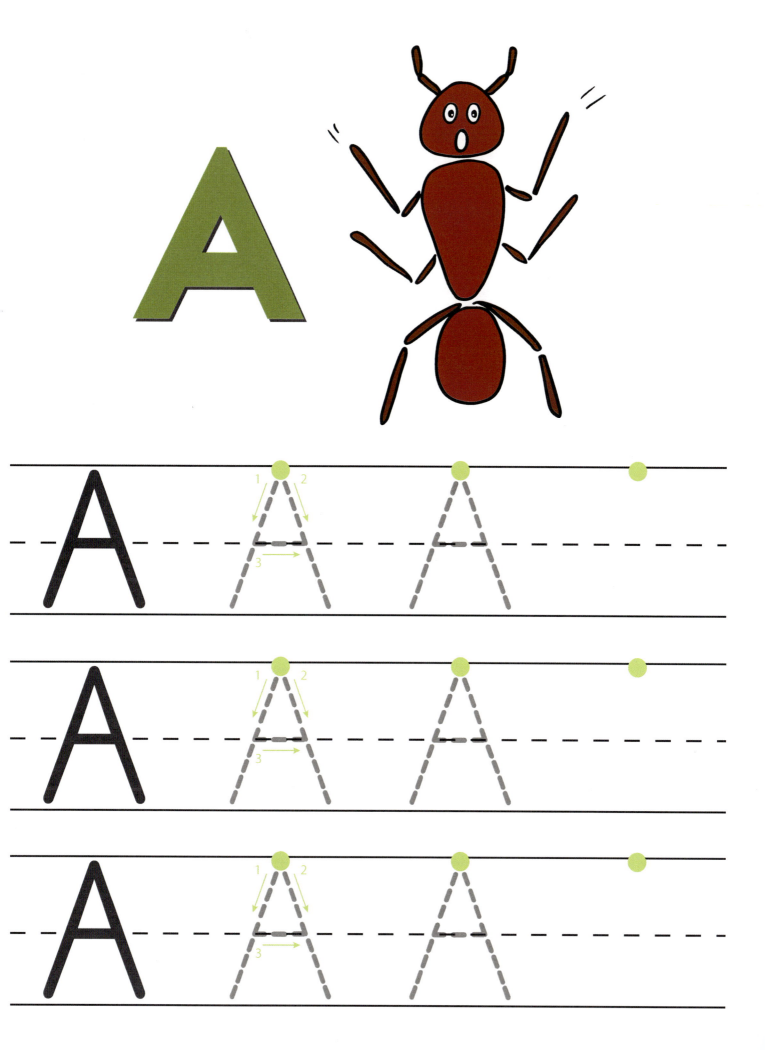

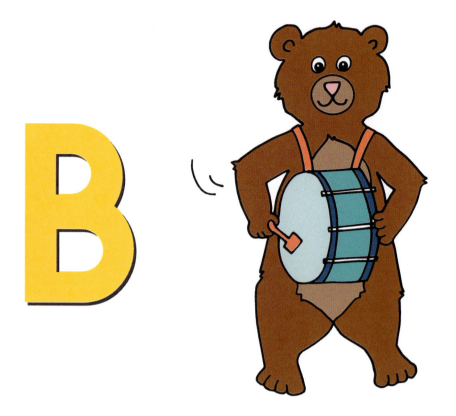

B   B   B   B

B   B   B   B

B   B   B   B

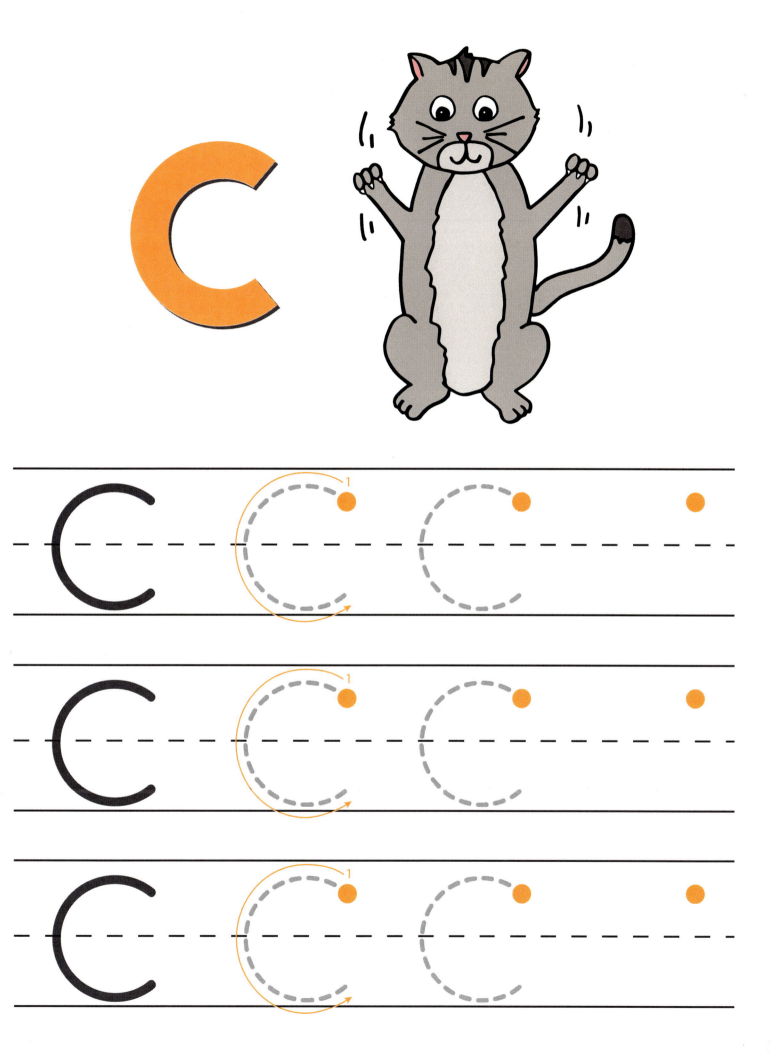

D

D D D D

D D D D

D D D D

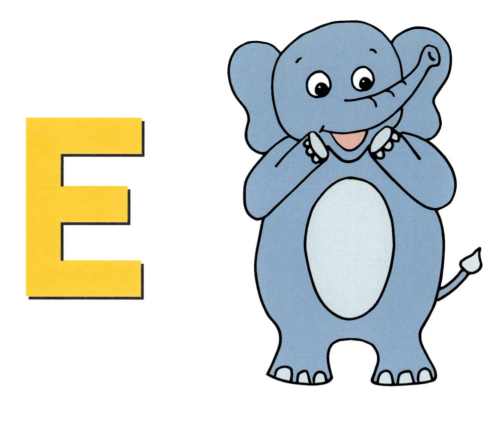

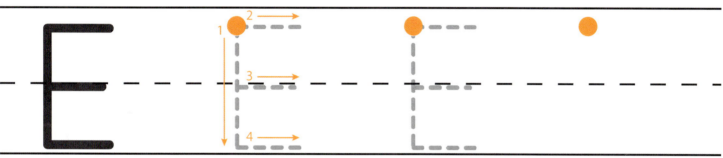

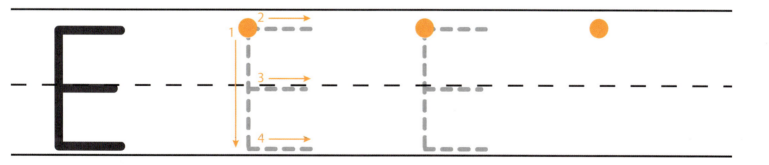

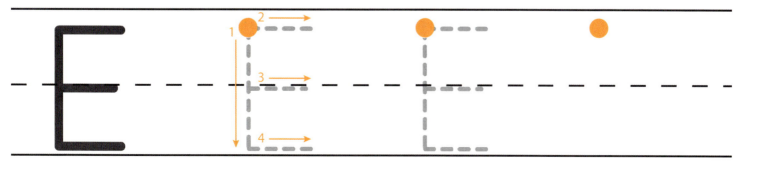

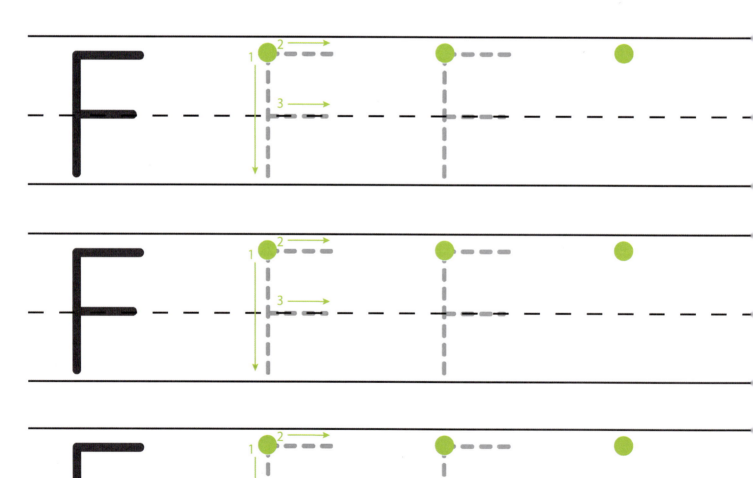

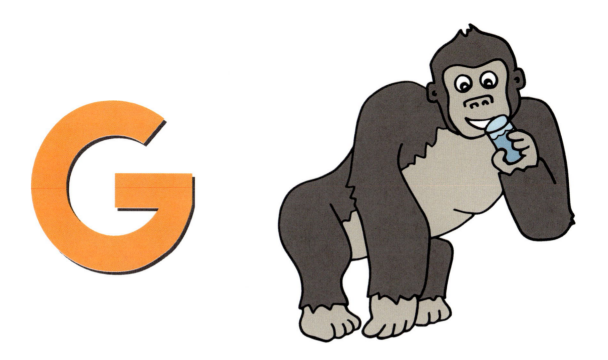

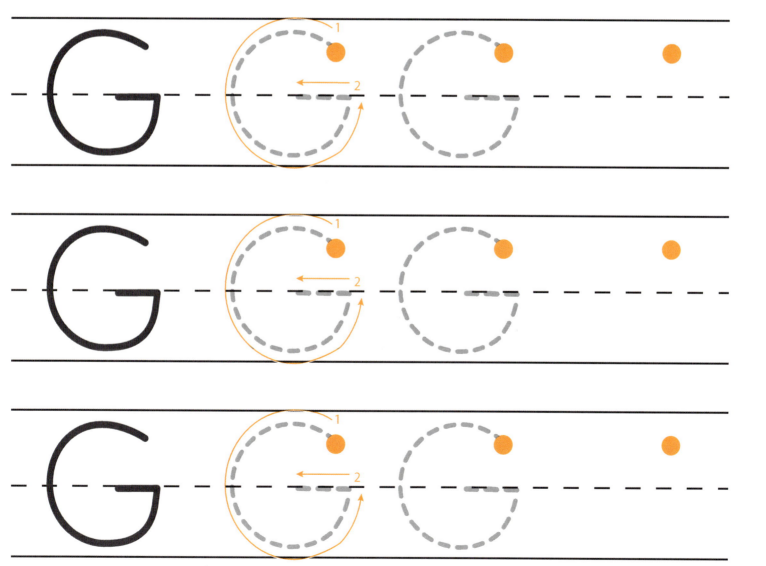

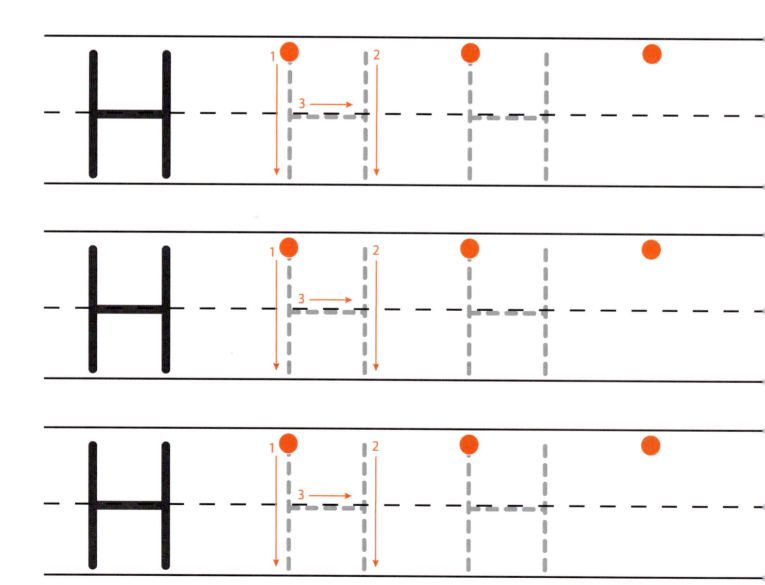

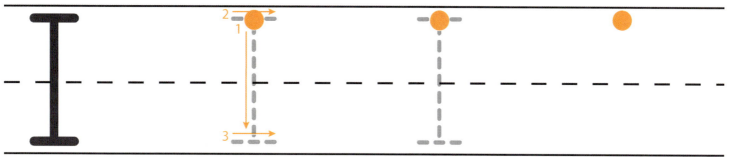

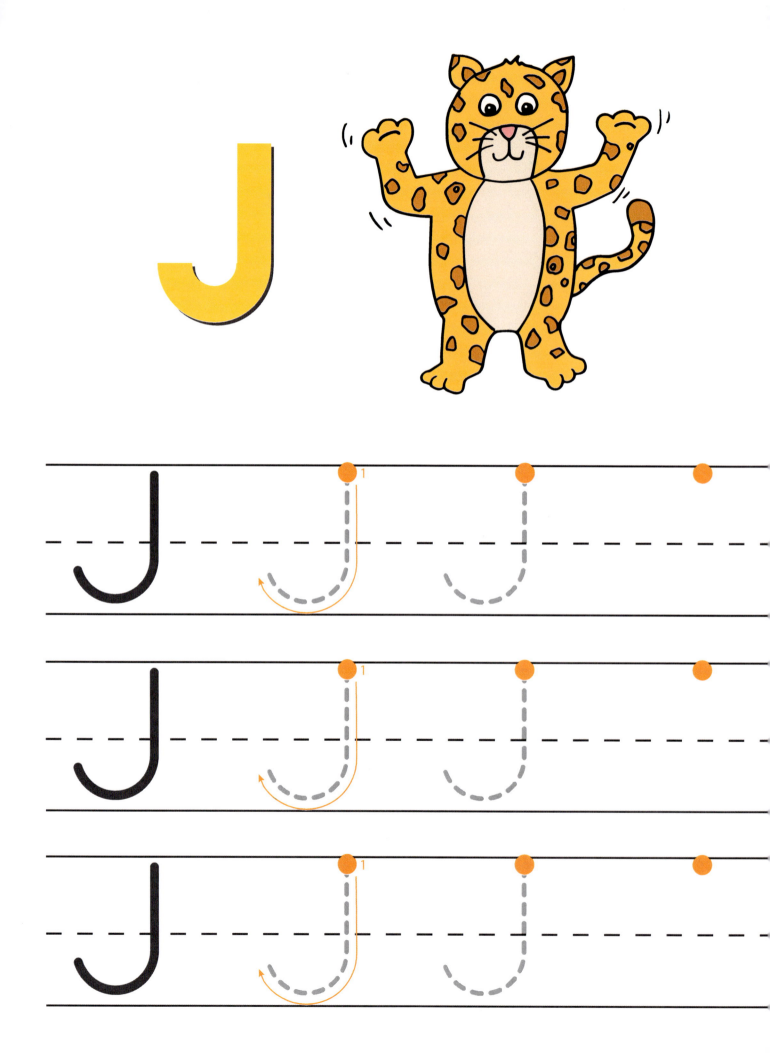

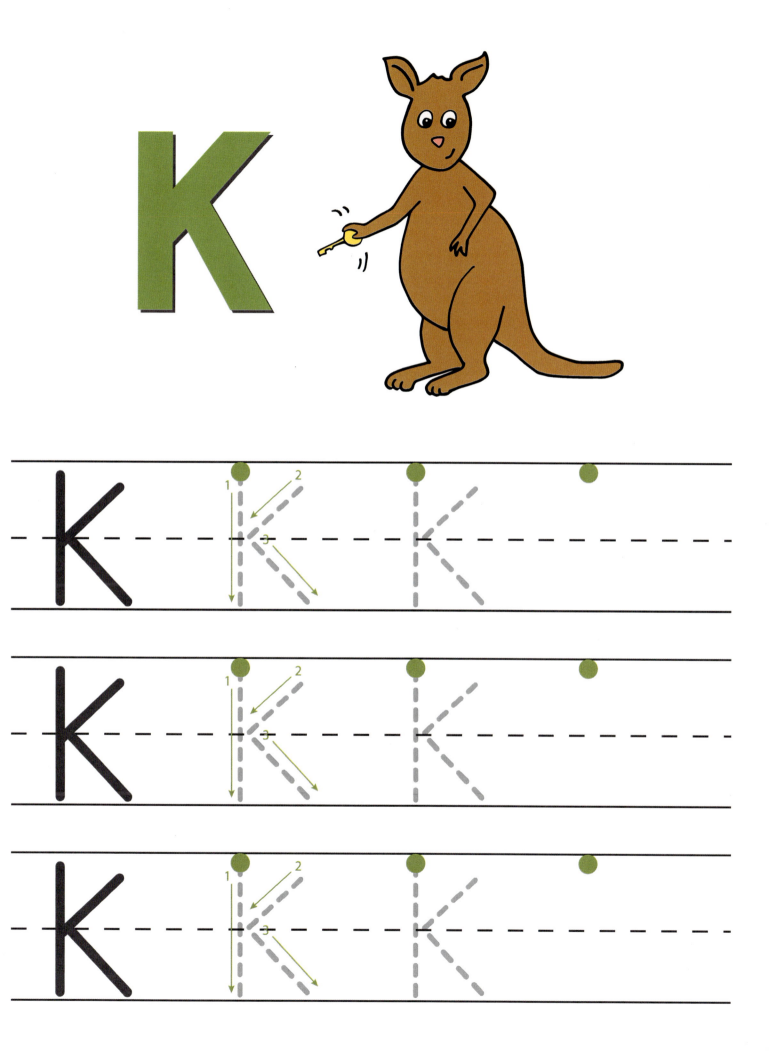

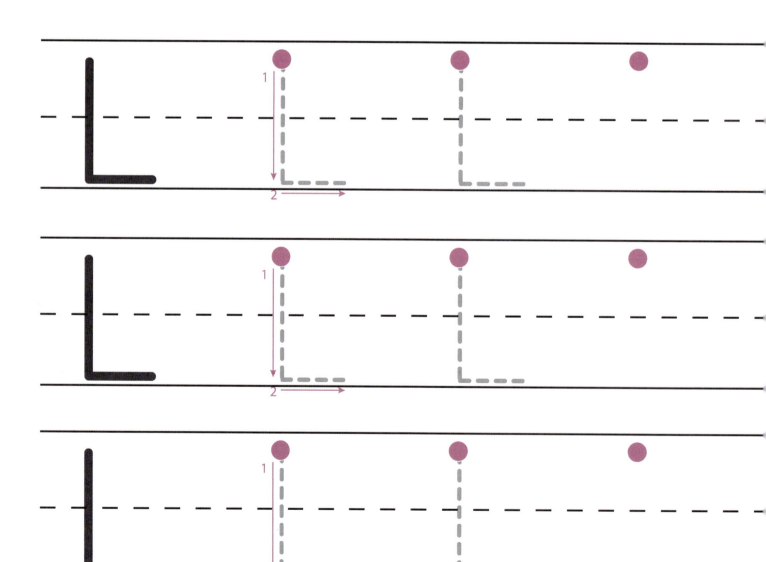

M

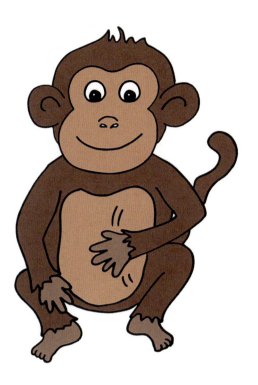

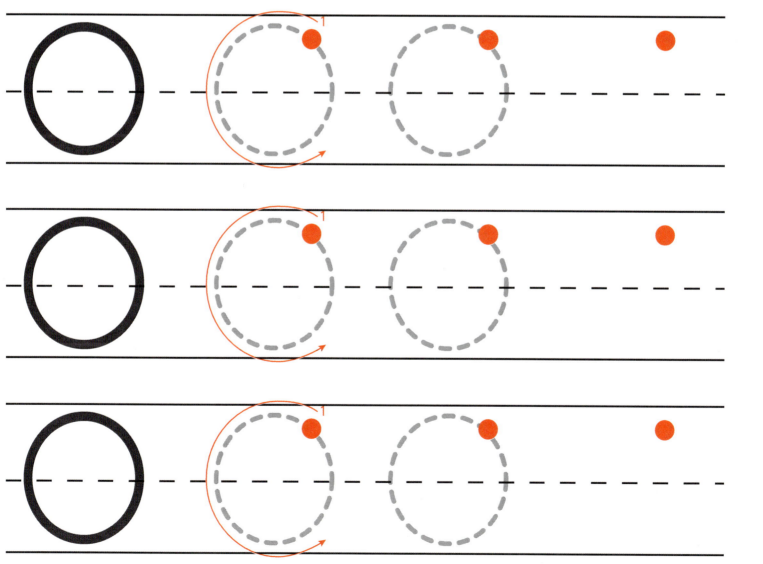

P

P P P

P P P

P P P

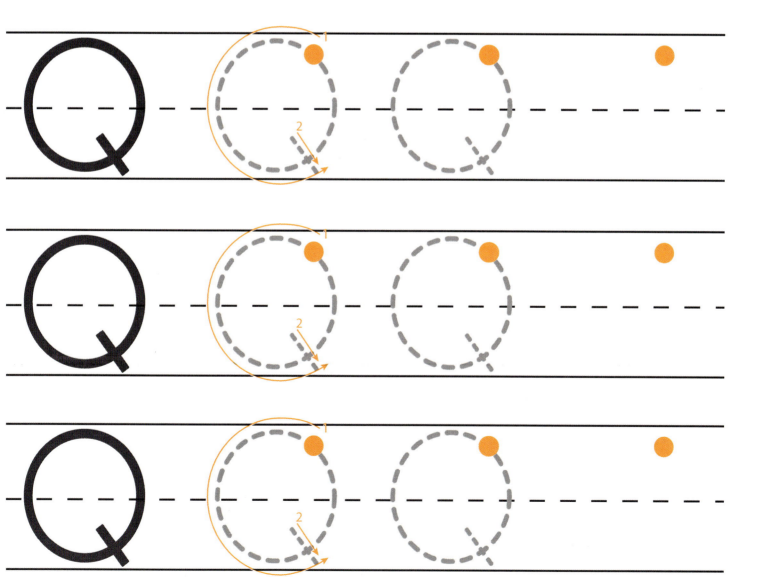

R

R   R   ²R   R
      1↓ 3↗

R   R   ²R   R
      1↓ 3↗

R   R   ²R   R
      1↓ 3↗

S

S   s   s   s

S   s   s   s

S   s   s   s

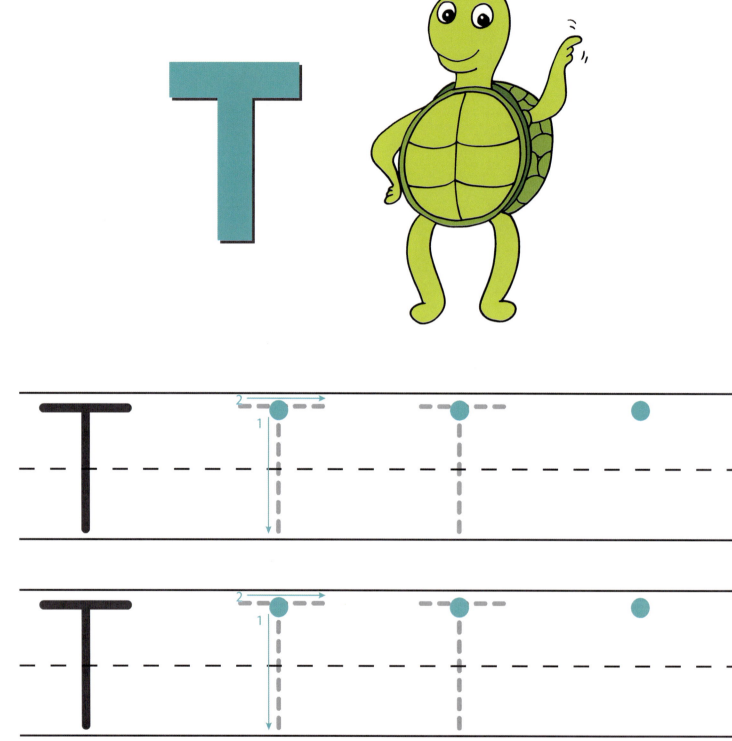

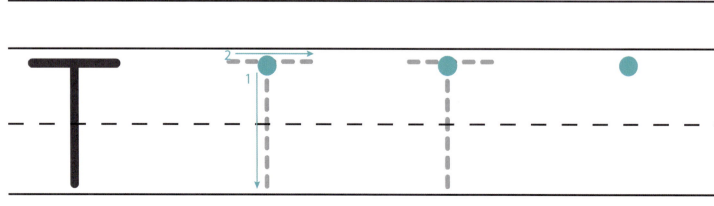

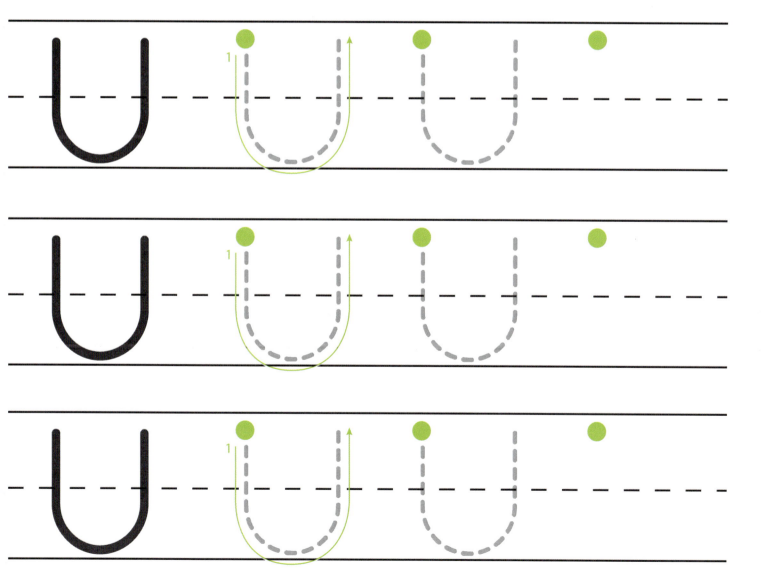

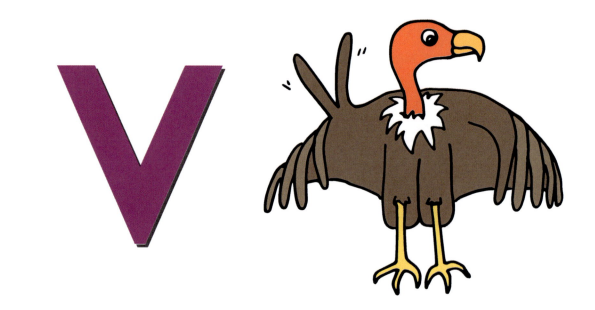

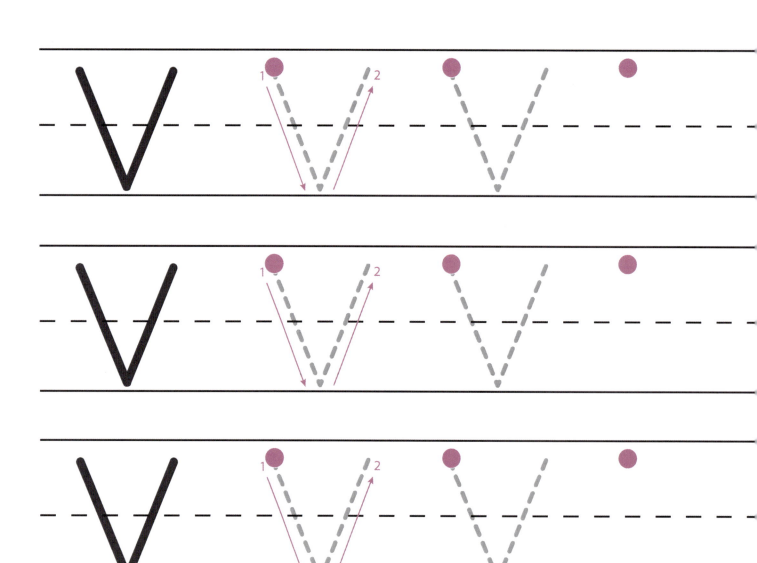

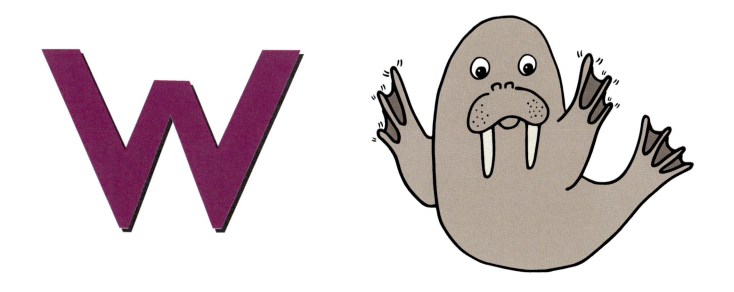

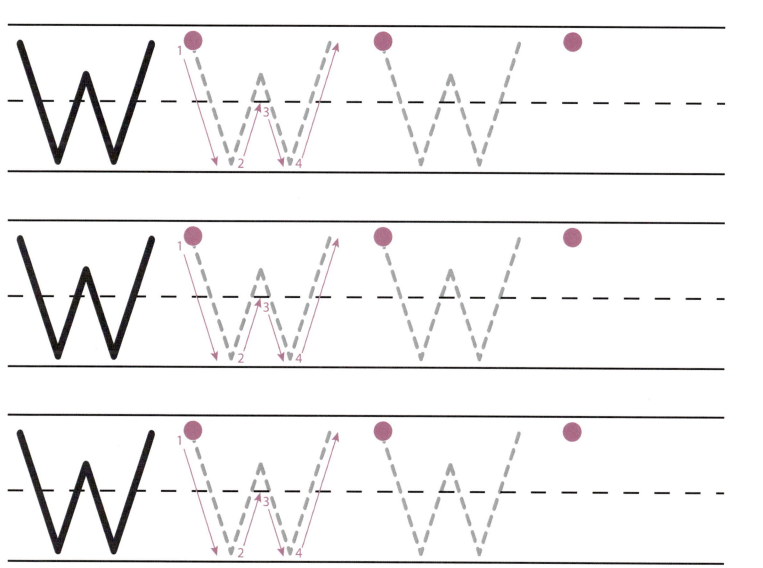

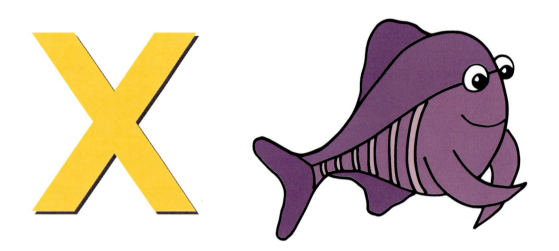

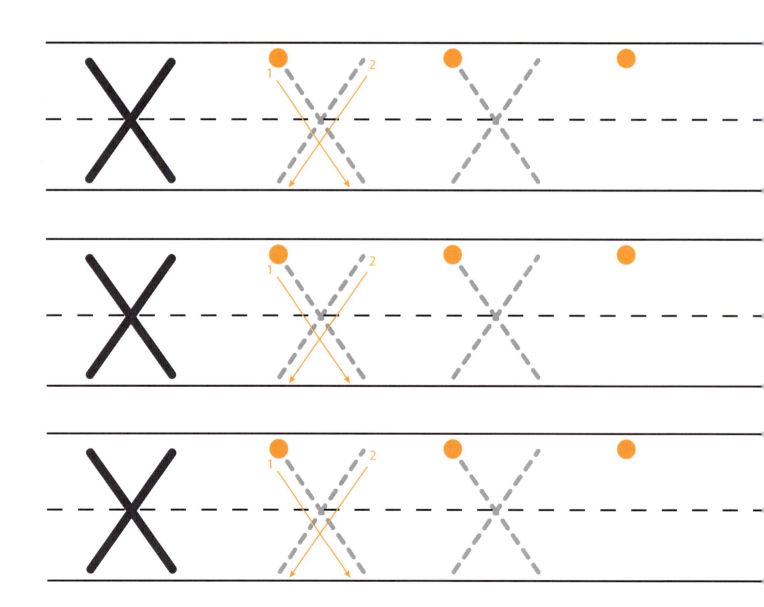

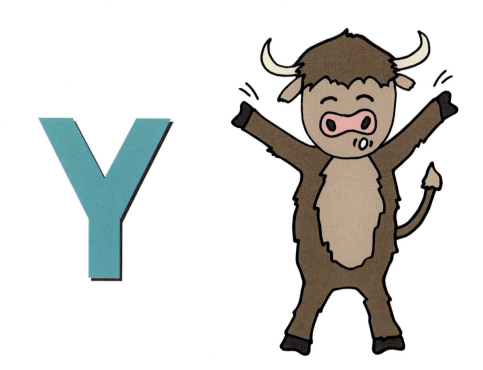

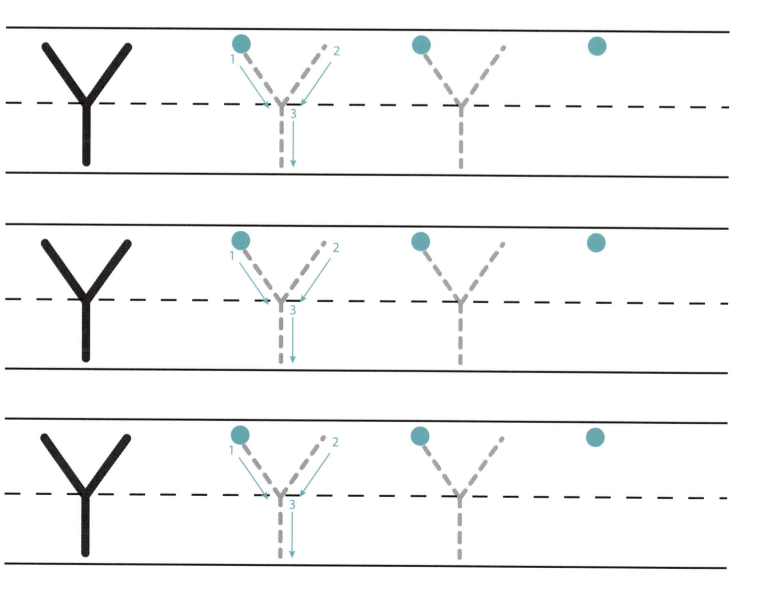

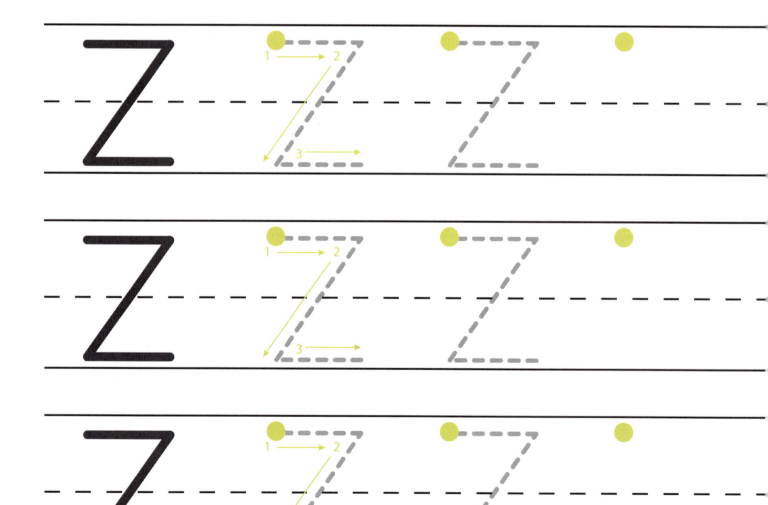

Made in the USA
Coppell, TX
29 June 2021